Calming Mandala

Coloring Book

Sweet Treats Edition

Illustrator - Joseph Rabie
Publisher - Evard Publishing

www.calmingmandala.com
www.evardpublishing.com

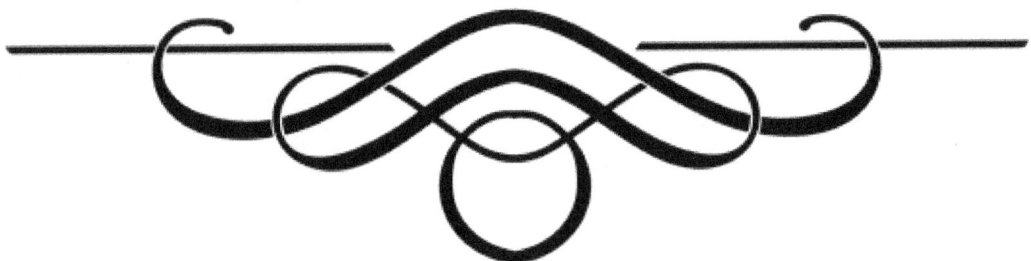

This Book Belongs to:

....

Lollipops

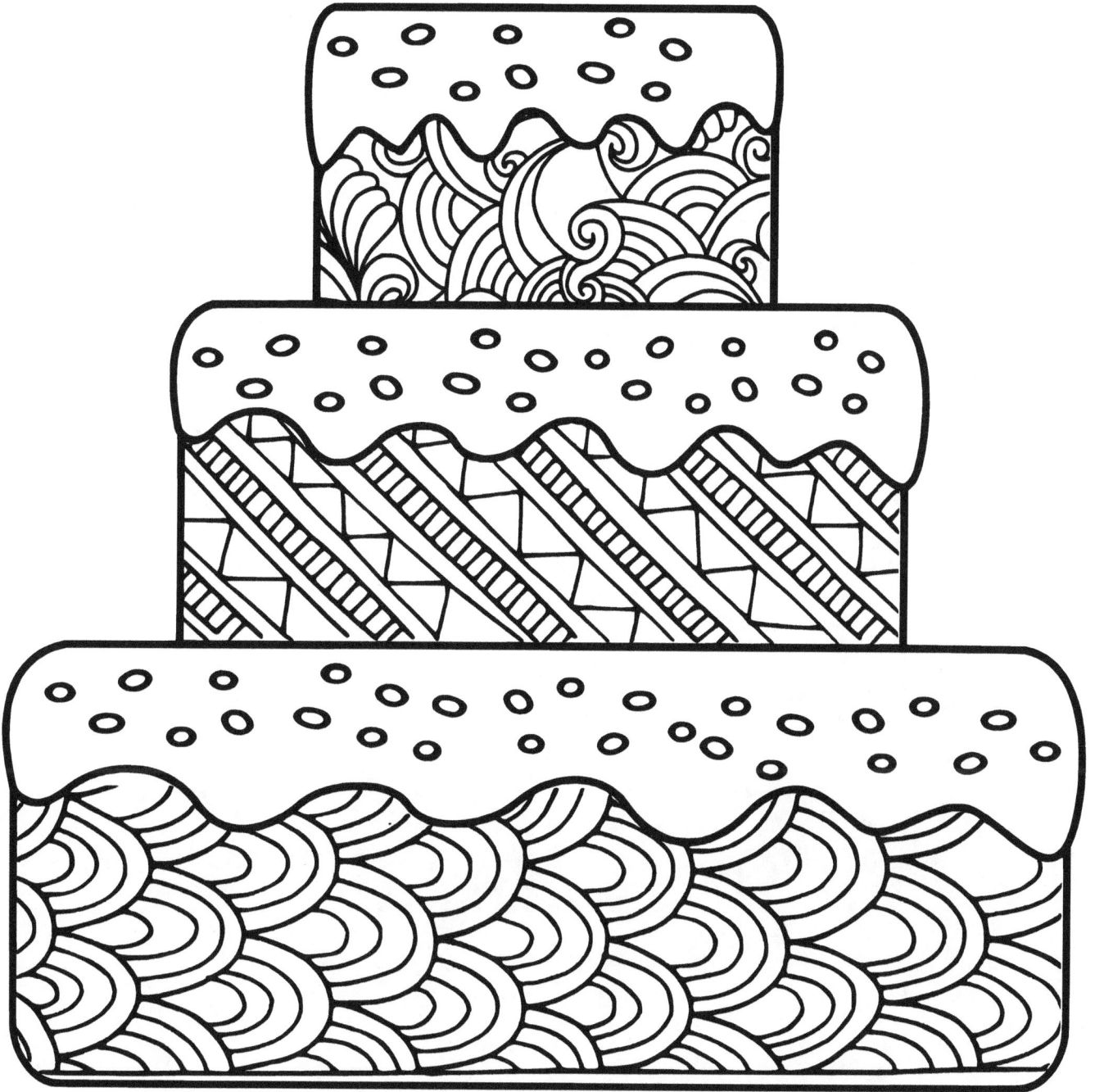

www.ingramcontent.com/pod-product-compliance
Lightning Source LLC
Chambersburg PA
CBHW081257040426

42452CB00014B/2541